MOMMY NEEDS A FREAKIN' BREAK

By Buster Gutt

Copyright © 2025 by Buster Gutt

All rights reserved.

No part of this book may be reproduced, distributed, or transmitted in any form or by any means, including photocopying, recording, or other electronic or mechanical methods, without the prior written permission of the author, except in the case of brief quotations embodied in critical reviews and certain other non-commercial uses permitted by copyright law.

Dedicated to all the Amazing Moms
who have too many jobs

Executive Chef, On-Call Nurse, Chauffeur, Laundry Technician, Event Planner, Therapist, Referee, IT Support, Search & Rescue Team, Personal Assistant, Fashion Consultant, Sleep Scientist, Home Decor Specialist, Budget Analyst, Motivational Speaker, Lie Detector, Logistics Coordinator, Creative Director, Disaster Recovery Specialist, Love and Hug Machine
& many more...

I thought at the start,
of this parenting journey,

this job would be
so easy.

How to NOT PARENT LIKE YOUR MOTHER

All pregnant, glowing with radiant skin.

Then boom!

I came over
all queasy!

Giving birth was a horrible, nightmare ordeal.

Now I'm forever **AWAKE!**

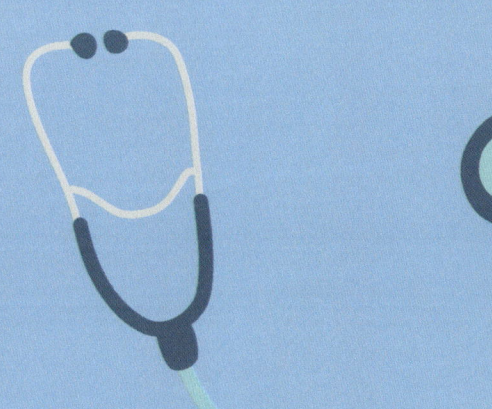

Then you finally slept, looking peacefully calm.
Surely now Mommy can have a small b r e a k ?

As I cook and I sip, my rancid, stale coffee.
I hear a deafening moan.

Mommy just needs, a bathroom break to herself.
Why can't you all leave me alone?

Eat and stop staring, at your cold, untouched plate.
I wanted you in bed **by** seven.

The day you can cook, your own edible meals, will be my idea of such heaven.

**No! I can't carry you, all flippin' day long.
Use your own legs, and walk.**

Please don't keep going on, and on at me now.
All you do is just non-stop TALK.

I don't have my own, social life anymore.
I don't see my friends, for Pete's sake.

We used to laugh, have fun and let *loose.*
Mommy just needs a weekend break.

I don't give two hoots, about the big Lego store.
Or going to Toys R Us.

But luckily there's a huge, Starbucks next door.
Which is always a **real big plus.**

I really don't care, who started it now.
Please just get on with your brother.

This constant moaning, is driving me

INSANE.

Why can't you get on with each other?

Why do you challenge, everything that I ask?
Please do what I SAY.

Because I said so, and don't you argue with me. I'm not in the **mood** today.

Do I look like an endless, ATM to you then?
I'm not giving you **anymore.**

You're reckless, you buy the most ridiculous stuff, when you go to that preppy store.

But I **LOVE** you, from the very bottom of my heart.

I'll be sad when you soon leave the nest.

But be most assured, I'll be fine when you go.
Because Mommy now needs that rest.

Mommy really needs, just one five-minute break!
I'm getting **very,**

very

tired.

If you don't like my tone, clean up your own mess

That's it. I'm done. I'm retired!

Now I'm ancient, alone, thinking of good old days.
I cry as I lie there awake.

Because finally, at last, the time has now come... for Mommy to have her **freakin' break!**

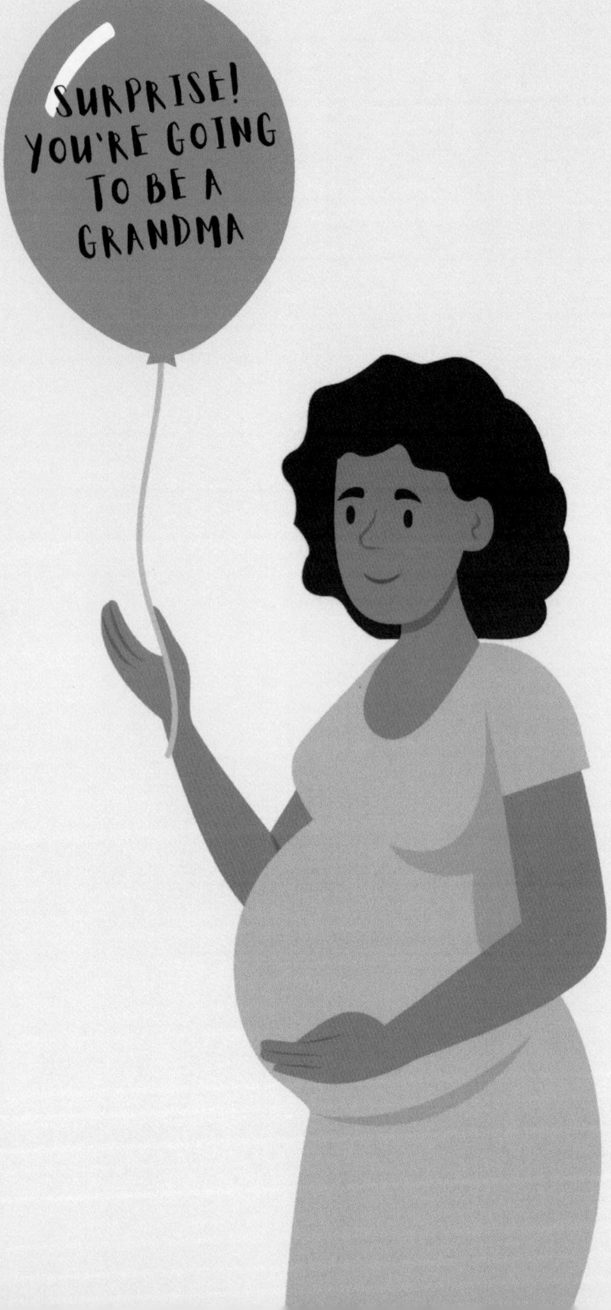
SURPRISE!
YOU'RE GOING
TO BE A
GRANDMA

Printed in Great Britain
by Amazon